ANIMALS TO
RESCUE!

Balto

WRITTEN BY
Emma Carlson Berne

ILLUSTRATED BY
Francesca Rosa

SCHOLASTIC PRESS ❖ NEW YORK

All rights reserved. Published by Scholastic Press, an imprint of Scholastic Inc., *Publishers since 1920.* SCHOLASTIC, SCHOLASTIC PRESS, and associated logos are trademarks and/or registered trademarks of Scholastic Inc.

The publisher does not have any control over and does not assume any responsibility for author or third-party websites or their content.

Library of Congress Cataloging-in-Publication Data Available

ISBN 978-1-338-68142-0 (paperback) / ISBN 978-1-338-68143-7 (library binding)

10 9 8 7 6 5 4 3 2 1   22 23 24 25 26

Printed in China   62
First edition, August 2022

Book design by Jaime Lucero

Table of Contents

A Hero Is Born

NOME, ALASKA

EARLY 1920s

Balto twisted his neck to look at the strange leather straps on his belly. Another strap was fastened tightly across his chest. He chewed at it.

"Leave it!" Sled dog driver Leonhard

Seppala's voice commanded. Balto snapped to attention.

Balto was only a puppy, but today he was wearing a sled dog harness for the very first time. He was going to run with the team. Leonhard clipped Balto in beside an experienced female dog. She would show the puppy what to do.

Leonhard stepped onto the sled behind the team. "Hike!" he shouted. The team surged forward with Balto right beside them.

In the 1920s, sled dogs were the most important animals in Nome, Alaska—almost as important as the people. During the summer, Nome depended on ships coming in and out of the harbor with supplies. In the winter months, the harbors iced over and stopped ships from traveling so far north. Planes had open cockpits and couldn't fly in snowstorms. The roads were buried in snow that was impossible for even teams of horses to travel on.

From fall to spring, the only way into Nome was over the Iditarod Trail. The trail stretched 938 miles from the port of Seward in the south, over mountains and through valleys, to Nome.

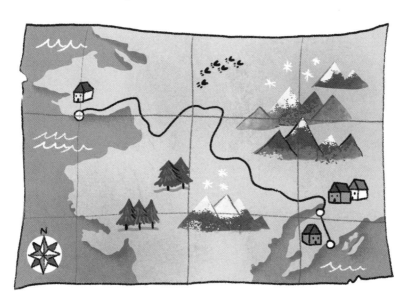

Without teams of sled dogs and their drivers, the town would be cut off from the rest of the world during the long winter months.

Balto was born to be a sled dog. He was a Siberian husky, one of the most common types of sled dog at that time. Malamutes were another popular sled dog breed. They were stronger than huskies, but slow. Malamutes would get into fights with other dogs, but huskies liked working in a group.

Huskies were smart.

They loved people.

And they loved to go.

Sled dog drivers made sure their teams were happy. An unhappy team could refuse to move—or even run away. And out on the trail, with the wind whistling over the ice, this could mean disaster for the team and the driver.

Sled dog puppies like Balto might start their training when they were only six or eight weeks old. They would run loose beside a grown-up sled dog team. The puppies would learn by watching how the adult dogs acted, and they would get used to running on snow, rocks, and ice. Some puppies would even try to wedge themselves into the team before they were put in a harness. When they were around nine months old, the pups would be strapped into the line for the first time.

To drive a sled dog team, the driver used only his or her voice. Balto and other young sled dogs already knew basic dog commands, like "sit" and "stay." During the training runs, Leonhard would teach them the commands for pulling a sled. "Hike" meant "go." "Whoa" was "stop." "Gee" meant "turn right," and "haw" meant "turn left."

The young sled dogs also needed to find out where they fit on the team. Every dog had a job. Wheel dogs were harnessed closest to the sled. They pulled and steered, so they had to be strong and steady. Swing dogs and team dogs ran in front of the wheel dogs. They added extra power and speed.

The lead dogs ran at the front. A team might have one or two lead dogs. Lead dogs were natural pilots. They had to follow directions, but they also had to think for themselves. If a driver gave a command that would put a team in danger, the lead dog needed to be confident enough to disobey.

Leonhard had many sled dogs. Some hauled sleds of supplies or other goods, but only the very best earned a place on Leonhard's racing team. This team included some of the smartest and fastest dogs in Nome—but it didn't

WHEEL DOGS

TEAM DOGS

SWING DOGS

LEAD DOG

include Balto. Leonhard thought a good racing sled dog should be sleek and slender. Balto's body was boxy and his legs looked bowed.

So when Balto was about six months old, Leonhard sent him to work at the Hammon Consolidated Gold Fields Company. The mining company used Leonhard's well-trained dogs to pull freight sleds loaded with gold and other supplies. Balto was a strong, quiet, willing dog, but he wasn't a leader. No one thought he ever would be.

CHAPTER 2

A Man and His Dog

Leonhard Seppala was one of the most famous sled dog drivers in Nome, Alaska. Born in Norway in 1877, he'd moved to Nome during the gold rush and started working as a sled dog driver for a mining company. It wasn't long before Leonhard began raising and training sled dogs of his own.

Leonhard Seppala's lead dog and partner was named Togo. At first, Leonhard thought Togo was wrong for a racing team, just like Balto. Togo had been a sick, runty puppy, and Leonhard decided he was too small. He gave him away to someone else as a pet.

But Togo didn't want to be a pet. He escaped from his new owner's house by jumping through a window and racing back to Leonhard. Impressed, Leonhard decided to keep him.

Togo started hanging around the other sled dogs. He would follow them on their runs, teasing and harassing them when they were on the trail. One day, Leonhard was so tired of Togo's games that he harnessed him to the team. Togo ran all day, and Leonhard saw that he was fast and focused. Eventually Togo earned the spot of lead dog.

Together, Togo and Leonhard were a racing machine. Leonhard said that Togo had won more races than any other dog in Alaska. But Togo was more than a racing dog to Leonhard. He was

Leonhard's friend, too. At night, they sat by the fire together. They liked to play a game where Leonhard would try to grab Togo's feet while the dog frolicked around.

By the time Togo was twelve, he and Leonhard had traveled nearly 55,000 miles of trail together. Leonhard trusted Togo more than any other dog. When the team crossed a stretch of ocean covered with sea ice, Leonhard would let Togo run ahead on a long rope. That way, Togo could choose the best route to travel on.

One day, out on a section of frozen ocean called the Norton Sound, Togo had a chance to prove just how smart and dedicated he was. Leonhard was driving his team out on the ice-covered Sound, with Togo in the lead. Storm winds started to blow and the ice began breaking into ice rafts, called "floes." Leonhard and his team found themselves alone on an ice floe, drifting in the middle of the Sound. Though they were not far from land, they were stuck. Dark, frigid water lapped at the edges of their icy raft. Finally, after several hours, the floe drifted close to the solid block of ice attached to the shore.

Thinking fast, Leonhard picked Togo up, attached him to a towline, and threw him onto the shore ice. Togo could drag the floe closer to shore so Leonhard and the team could get across. Togo understood immediately. He dug his feet in and pulled, the towline stretching tight.

Then the line snapped. One end flipped into the water. Togo was on the shore ice. Leonhard and the rest of the team were on the floe. Freezing water separated them and the shore. They were trapped.

But Togo wasn't going to give up. He would do anything for Leonhard. Togo jumped into the water and grabbed the broken towline with his teeth. He scrambled back onto the shore ice, lay down, and rolled over, looping

the towline over his own shoulders. Standing, he lowered his head and pulled. The ice floe began to move. Togo pulled harder. The floe floated closer and closer until Leonhard and the other dogs could safely step onto shore. Togo had saved the team. Leonhard was sure no other dog could have done it.

Leonhard had no idea that one day Togo would be running to save the lives of more than his team or his leader. He would be running to save the lives of the children of Nome.

Sickness Spreads!

NOME, ALASKA
1925

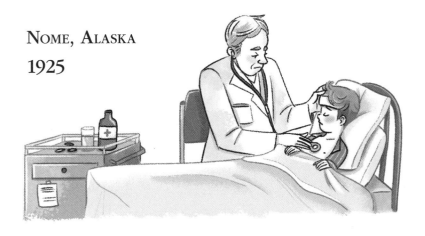

Three-year-old Billy Barnett was very sick. His glands were swollen and he had a high fever. Scariest of all, a thick, grayish film was slowly growing across the back of his throat.

Dr. Curtis Welch straightened up from Billy's bedside at Maynard Columbus Hospital and swallowed hard. Billy had a disease called "diphtheria," and Dr. Welch was very worried. He was the only doctor in Nome, and he was looking at a possible disaster.

Diphtheria was deadly. It was very contagious and was passed from person to person through coughing or sneezing. It could live on objects, like doorknobs, clothes, and toys. It also infected children more than adults.

Dr. Welch knew that if Billy had diphtheria, then other children in town must have it, too. Christmas had just passed. The whole town had celebrated together—which also meant they were breathing on one other, coughing, and sharing mittens.

Now diphtheria was lurking among the town's children. Alaska Native children were especially in danger. Their bodies had very little immunity to the disease. If they got sick, they were more likely to die.

There was a cure. Diphtheria antitoxin was a medicine that came in the form of a serum. The antitoxin serum would halt the disease.

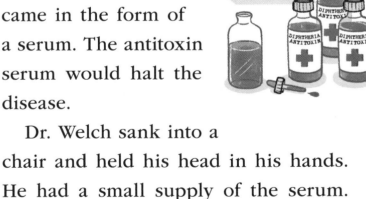

Dr. Welch sank into a chair and held his head in his hands. He had a small supply of the serum. He knew where it was—right in his medicine storeroom—but the serum had expired and no longer worked. Dr. Welch had ordered a fresh supply over the summer, but it had never been delivered. Now the town was iced in. No ships were docking in the harbor, and that meant no serum was coming in, either.

Billy Barnett died a short time later. By the next evening, seven-year-old Alaska Native Bessie Stanley had died, too.

The diphtheria outbreak had begun.

*   *   *

Dr. Welch ordered that the town be placed under quarantine. The town leaders held an emergency meeting. They needed more serum— fast. Anchorage might have some they could share. It was one of the biggest cities in Alaska and had well-stocked hospitals. But how was Nome going to get it? The harbors would not melt for months, there were no trains to Nome, and every road was buried in snow.

They might be able to fly it in. But airplanes had just begun flying in Alaska. They were rickety and crashed all the time. They also had an open cockpit, which meant the flight was dangerously cold during the winter. No one had ever flown across the inner land of Alaska in January.

There was one other way to get supplies into Nome—by dogsled. All winter long, the dogsled mail teams pulled their cargo down Front Street, fresh from the Iditarod Trail. These mail teams were made up of the fastest sled dogs in Alaska and were driven by the best drivers.

The town leaders agreed. Dogs were Nome's partners. The mail teams were Nome's heroes. And now, they just might save the lives of Nome's children.

Dr. Welch sent a telegram to Anchorage and another to the U.S. Public Health Service. Nome did not have long-distance telephones, so telegrams were the only way to send an urgent message to the outside world. With a series of clicks that matched up to letters, the message could be sent through radio waves. "I am in urgent need of one million units of diphtheria antitoxin," Dr. Welch wrote.

The message soon came back. 300,000 units of antitoxin serum had been located. It would be enough to stop the spread of the disease until more units could be found.

The town leaders formed a plan. The serum would be packaged and loaded onto a train in Anchorage. It would be sent to the very end of the railroad line, to a town called Nenana. A sled dog mail team would meet the train there. The serum would then be carried by a relay. Each sled dog team would travel thirty miles before handing the package off to the next driver. The teams would race around the clock to reach Nome. The relay should take about five days.

The trip would be perilous. A blizzard was forming along the trail. The dogs could lose the trail in snowy conditions and slide off cliffs, taking the sled with them. And the temperature was expected to plunge to sixty degrees below zero at night. In that kind of cold, drivers could freeze while trying to start a fire. A driver could lose a hand just by taking off a glove to wipe ice from a dog's paws. The dogs would be traveling on dark paths in winds that were so powerful they could knock an entire team off their feet. Despite these dangers, the teams were Nome's only hope.

CHAPTER
4

The Mission

The call went out and the telegraph wires hummed with the message. In cabins all along the Iditarod Trail, drivers answered the call.

Far away in Anchorage, a doctor named John Beeson wrapped the glass bottles of serum in a quilt. He nestled the bottles inside a sturdy wooden crate. Then he wrapped the crate in heavy brown cloth. The serum bottles needed to be warm and protected during the long journey.

Back in Nome, drivers stood in the blowing snow and looked over their teams. They would take only the best and the fastest dogs. Every minute counted. Hundreds of dogs began yipping and barking in a rising chorus. They were ready to go.

Of the drivers who would make the journey, fourteen were Alaska Natives. Sam Joseph was from the Tanana peoples. Titus Nikolai and Jack "Jackscrew" Nicolai were Dene Athabascan from Interior Alaska, as were Johnny Folger, Edgar Kallands, brothers George and Edgar Nollner,

Harry Pitka, and Dave Corning. Charlie Evans was from Galena, Alaska, and Tommy Patson was from Nulato, Alaska. Both were Koyukon Athabascan. Finally, Victor Anagick, Myles Gonangnan, and Henry Ivanoff were Inuit (or Inupiaq).

Twenty drivers and 150 dogs would carry the serum on the relay. Usually, these teams pulled sleds loaded with mail, tools, and groceries. On this journey, they would pull only the serum crate. The lighter sled would allow them to travel more quickly over the snow.

The relay was broken into roughly equal distances—about thirty miles per driver. Only one driver was assigned a longer route. Leonhard Seppala would be a part of this relay. He would travel three times the distance of the other drivers—over ninety miles. He was the best driver in Alaska and he had the best team. If anyone could do it, Leonhard could.

Leonhard probably wasn't thinking of Balto at all as he prepared for the journey. The dog wasn't even at Leonhard's own kennel. He was miles away at the kennels of the Hammon Consolidated Gold Fields Company.

Togo would lead Leonhard's team of nineteen dogs. Togo was twelve years old, which was old for a sled dog, but Togo was the only dog Leonhard could trust to lead his team on such an important mission.

Togo was going to need every bit of

his trail speed and strength. Some parts of Alaska were among the coldest places on the planet. Danger was everywhere. Trees exploded from the cold. Water flowed out from frozen rivers and made huge puddles on the surface of the ice. A driver and dog team who got wet might freeze to death before the driver could build a fire.

Leonhard and Togo's part of the relay would take them over Norton Sound, the expanse of frozen ocean they had crossed many times before. Their team would run over miles of treacherous, shifting ice. If the ice broke up when they were in the middle of the Sound, they would fall in and the serum would be lost.

In the protected yard of Leonhard's cabin, the light spilled cozily from the windows onto the snow. The dogs were bedded down snugly in their kennels. They were nestled deep in straw, curled into furry balls with their tails wrapped around their noses. Leonhard crouched next to Togo's kennel. The dog looked up at him, his eyes calm and understanding, and laid his ears back. "Ready to run, partner?" Leonhard asked. Togo gazed back.

Leonhard scratched Togo and stood up. He and Togo had traveled this trail too many times to count. This might be the old dog's last run. It would also be the most dangerous.

CHAPTER 5

The Team

Gunnar Kaasen was a quiet, serious man. Like many people living in Alaska, he had come from Norway in search of gold. He didn't find very much gold, but he did discover a love for sled dogs. He and Leonhard worked together at the Hammon Consolidated Gold Fields Company. Gunnar knew the dog teams at Hammon well.

Now the call had come in. Gunnar was taking the second-to-last leg of the relay. He would travel to the roadhouse in Bluff, where he would wait for the serum. He would then transport the medicine from Bluff to the roadhouse in Port Safety, thirty-four miles away, and pass the serum to the final driver.

The blizzard was already brewing outside. The trail would soon be covered in snow drifts. Drivers usually stopped during a blizzard and waited out the winds. But Gunnar and his team were going to run in the storm, at night, on an unfamiliar trail.

They would have to cross the frozen Topkok River and climb over the ridges that ran along its banks. Then they would run up Topkok Mountain, six hundred feet tall. Gunnar knew that the wind at the summit would be brutal. They would be in total darkness. One misstep and the driver and team could plunge off the cliffs to the ocean below.

Gunnar went out to the Hammon company kennels. Leonhard had given

Gunnar instructions before he left. Gunnar was to use an experienced dog named Fox for his lead if he needed a team while Leonhard was gone. Standing in the snowy yard with the winds whipping around him, Gunnar looked over the dogs.

Billy, Sye, Tillie, Alaska Slim, Moctoc—Gunnar began clipping the dogs into the line. One by one, he wrestled the dogs into their harnesses as they barked and jumped, wild to begin racing.

Now for the lead dog. Brown-and-black Fox gazed up at Gunnar expectantly. He'd been the lead dog many times. He knew what to do. But then Gunnar looked over at a sturdy black dog.

Balto stood pressed against the

edge of his kennel, his eyes bright. He was steady, big, and powerful. But he had mainly pulled sleds on short runs over routes he already knew. He didn't have years of experience on unfamiliar trails, racing at top speeds for miles at a time. Not like Togo. Not like Fox. Still, there was something about Balto that Gunnar liked.

For one moment, Leonhard's instructions echoed in Gunnar's head. "If you need a lead, use Fox." Then Gunnar pushed Leonhard's words away. He opened the kennel door and pressed the other dogs back with his knee. "Balto, come!" he commanded. Balto bounded forward, his mouth open, tongue hanging out. Gunnar clipped Balto into place at the head of the line. For the first time, Balto was the lead dog.

The winds were cutting through Gunnar's fur parka. The dogs were well protected at least—huskies like Balto had two fur coats: The downy undercoat was like insulation. Close to the skin, it was thick and fluffy to trap the dog's body heat. The outer coat was waterproof, with long, coarse hairs that kept ice away from the body. Huskies could keep their body heat in almost any weather. Gunnar checked the supplies in his pack. Chunks of salmon and tallow—beef fat—filled the inside. His dogs would need all that high-calorie protein to keep them warm and give them energy on the trail.

Gunnar stepped onto the back of the sled. The dogs danced on their lines. At the front, Balto stood tall, every muscle in his body ready to go. "Hike!" Gunnar shouted. Balto leaned into his harness and pulled. The other dogs followed. The sled started with a jerk before gliding out onto the trail. Gunnar, Balto, and twelve other Siberian huskies were on their way to save the children of Nome.

CHAPTER 6

The Journey Begins

ANCHORAGE, ALASKA

JANUARY 26, 1925

Dr. Beeson checked that the 300,000 units of diphtheria serum were secure in their crate. Then he wrote a note and pinned it to the package. It instructed the drivers to bring the serum inside at each stop and warm it up by the fire for fifteen minutes to keep it from freezing.

He hurried to the railway station. The

locomotive was waiting on the tracks, puffing steam. Dr. Beeson passed the precious crate to the train conductor. The train's whistle pierced the icy air and the train pulled out of the Anchorage station bound for Nenana, three hundred miles away.

Twenty-four hours later, at nine o'clock at night on Tuesday, January 27, the locomotive arrived at its destination. The first driver, Wild Bill

Shannon, was waiting on the platform. His dogs were harnessed and ready. The conductor ran the crate over to Wild Bill, who strapped it to his sled and triple-checked the lines. In front of a watching crowd, Wild Bill and his team sped out of Nenana, racing for their destination—the roadhouse at Tolovana. The relay had begun.

Wild Bill carried an axe, food, a tarp, a blanket, a knife, and matches. He also carried a load of worry. The temperature was already fifty degrees below zero. The dogs could be in danger at just forty degrees below, and the conditions were getting worse.

Wild Bill was also worried about his team's ability to complete the run. His lead dog, Blackie, was experienced and reliable, but his other dogs were young and inexperienced. They had never been on a long-distance run. They would try their hardest. Wild Bill had no doubt about that. But would it be enough?

The team hit trouble right away. A horse team had passed through a few days earlier and punched giant holes in the hard-packed snow that covered the trail. Holes like these were dangerous for the driver and the dogs. They could overturn the sled, and the sharp edges of the holes hurt the dogs' feet. Wild Bill swung the team to the left. They were

going to have to run on the slick ice of the Tanana River.

The frozen river was smooth and beautiful. But danger waited below its surface. Water could flow over the top of the ice and soak the dogs and the driver. Wet fur, feet, and boots were deadly at fifty degrees below zero.

As they ran through the dark, Wild Bill realized that he had another problem. The cold air itself was dangerous. Wild Bill was having trouble feeling his feet, and his face was numb. He began running beside the sled to warm himself, but still he grew colder and colder.

The dogs were almost too cold to keep going. They were slowing down and stumbling in the snow. Four of them had nosebleeds.

Wild Bill knew they couldn't survive much longer. Then he saw the warm orange lights of the Minto roadhouse ahead. They'd reached the halfway point to Tolovana.

Wild Bill stumbled to the roadhouse and into its sweet, smoky warmth. The dogs rested in a warm shed as Wild Bill gulped hot coffee. His face was black with frostbite, but he had not frozen. He was lucky.

Four hours later, Wild Bill harnessed up the team again. His dogs Cub, Jack, and Jet would remain behind since they were not well enough to keep running. The keeper at the roadhouse would take good care of them until Wild Bill's return.

At eleven o'clock in the morning on January 28, fourteen hours after he left Nenana, Wild Bill pulled into the Tolovana roadhouse. He'd completed the first leg of the relay. Exhausted, he unstrapped the crate and handed it over to Edgar Kallands.

Edgar ran his dogs through the heavy forests between Tolovana and his end point, Manley Hot Springs. The temperature was now fifty-six degrees below zero. When Edgar got off his sled at the end of his thirty-one-mile run, he found that his mittens had frozen to the sled's handlebar. Hot water had to

be poured over them. Edgar passed the serum to the next driver, Dan Green. Dan passed it to Johnny Folger. The teams ran all day and into the night.

The serum inched closer and closer to Nome. Johnny handed the precious crate to Sam Joseph. Sam passed it to Titus Nikolai. At each roadhouse stop, the drivers took the serum inside to warm it up, as Dr. Beeson had instructed.

Charlie Evans was the twelfth relay driver. At three o'clock in the morning on January 30, he took the serum from George Nollner. In the black night, Charlie could hear the boom of trees exploding from the cold. His dogs ran through a blinding ice fog. Charlie could barely see the edge of his sled, let alone the trail.

Then the wind picked up and his lead dogs started staggering. They were too cold to keep running.

Charlie unharnessed his lead dogs and put them in the sled. He stepped to the front of the line, picked up the harnesses, and threw the straps of leather over his own shoulders. Then he began to run.

CHAPTER 7

Darkness Falls

In Nome, Dr. Welch was trying to fight the outbreak, but the spread of the disease continued. The doctor was exhausted and heartsick. Would the serum make it in time?

Out on the trail, the medicine was being transferred slowly but surely from driver to driver. On January 31, Leonhard Seppala and Togo found driver Henry Ivanoff trying to keep his dogs from fighting a reindeer. Henry passed the serum over and Leonhard strapped it down tight in his sled. Togo and the dogs had already run 170 miles from Nome to reach the meeting point near Shaktoolik. Now the winds were nearing blizzard strength and darkness was falling. But no matter the weather, the team needed to cross the Norton Sound.

Driving across Norton Sound meant Leonhard, Togo, and the team would be out on open ice. The ice covering the Sound wasn't a solid, unmoving layer like a floor. It heaved and split and groaned and cracked. It could break apart at any moment. And the wind out on the Sound could reach seventy miles an hour. It could flip a dogsled and a team right over.

There was a trail around the Sound. It was safe, on solid land—but it was slow. Going around the Sound would add an entire day to the journey. Leonhard thought of the children lying ill in Nome and pushed his team forward.

Togo led the team through the dark and out onto the ice, head down and body straight and strong. Skillfully, he zigzagged around dangerous cracks. In the powerful wind, the temperature felt like eighty-five degrees below zero. But the ice held.

Finally, they returned to solid ground and pulled up to their first stop, the Isaac's Point roadhouse.

Safe inside the snug walls of the roadhouse, Leonhard could hear the wind rising outside. The blizzard was in full force. Hours later, fortified with coffee, salmon, and sleep, Leonhard and Togo led the team up and down the steep, exposed ridges of Little McKinley Mountain. Thirteen hours after leaving the roadhouse at Isaac's Point, Leonhard delivered the serum into the hands of Charlie Olson. His dogs had run 261 miles since leaving Nome. Togo had led them every step of the way. It was the old dog's last long-distance run. It was also his greatest.

*   *   *

On February 1, at seven o'clock in the evening, Charlie Olson and his team slid into the roadhouse at Bluff. They handed the serum off to the second-to-last driver in the relay: Gunnar Kaasen and his lead dog, Balto.

Charlie warned Gunnar about the storm. His own dogs had almost frozen

to death. Gunnar listened carefully, then made up his mind. If he waited, snowdrifts would pile up on the trail and they wouldn't be able to pass through for several more days. His dogs were ready. It was time to go.

Balto and Gunnar's route would take them from Bluff to the roadhouse at Port Safety. There, driver Ed Rohn would pick up the serum and complete the last leg into Nome. The team would rest partway through at the Solomon roadhouse. By then, Gunnar knew they would need it.

Outside in the howling blizzard, the cold bit through Gunnar's fur parka. Bracing against the wind, Gunnar knelt down beside his sturdy, bright-eyed lead dog. Balto stood straight and proud in his harness. He knew what his job was going to be. Balto licked Gunnar's chin. The other dogs howled behind them, competing with the shriek of the wind. They were ready to run.

Gunnar ran his hand over Balto's black head. He'd chosen Balto above all the rest. Now the team needed a strong leader to guide them through the storm. Gunnar only hoped he'd chosen the right dog.

CHAPTER 8

Balto Leads the Way

The thirteen-dog team plunged into the pitch-dark storm with Gunnar at the back, standing strong like a tree trunk against the wind. At the front of the pack, Balto had to navigate the way all lead dogs did—with his feet and his nose. His sensitive footpads told him that there was packed snow under the fresh powder. His powerful nose could sniff out the faintest scent of the dogs who had used the trail before, despite the screaming winds and whirling snow.

Balto kept the team on the path for five miles until a huge snow drift blocked their way. Balto plowed into it bravely, but the snow was too deep. The dogs were stuck. Fighting his way through the snow, Gunnar took hold of his lead dog's harness and pulled him in a tight half-circle out of the drift.

Now they had only one choice—to leave the trail and go around a ridge. This was a completely unknown stretch of land, and Balto wasn't used to going

off-trail. An experienced dog would know what to do. Was Balto up to the challenge?

Balto carefully guided the team around the dangerous ridge. One wrong step could mean disaster for the dogs and Gunnar. After several heart-pounding minutes, they finally made it around the drift and stepped off the ridge. Gunnar breathed a sigh of relief. They were safe, but now Balto had to find the trail again. The husky sniffed and sniffed, hesitantly padding forward. Suddenly, he leaned into his harness and pulled hard. They were back on the right path. Balto had done it.

Their next challenge was reaching the steep peak of Topkok Mountain. Up, up, the team pulled. Above them,

the mountain thrust its craggy face into the storm. The team strained up the slope, and Gunnar used pedals on the sled to help keep them moving. At last they reached the summit and stopped to take a breath. They'd made it, but Gunnar's relief lasted only a moment. The journey down would be just as dangerous. One wrong move on the high ridge would send them tumbling off the cliffs.

The team raced down the steep slope to the flats beyond. Balto led the dogs skillfully, avoiding drifts and keeping the sled solidly on the trail. Finally, they were off the mountain.

The storm was growing worse. Through the blustering snow, Gunnar could not even see the dogs closest to his sled. He stopped shouting commands. He couldn't trust his own judgement, and the dogs couldn't hear him over the howling wind anyway. Balto would need to lead the team through the blizzard alone.

They were almost to the Solomon roadhouse, where a fire would be crackling in the woodstove. There would be hot soup and coffee for Gunnar and salmon and a deep bed of straw for the dogs.

The team crossed beach flats caked with sea ice. Here, the ocean water reached into the land, covered by fresh snow. It was hard to tell where the beach ended and the ocean began. Balto could accidentally lead the team out onto the open, frozen sea. Violent winds funneled down the beach. The dogs' toes scrabbled on shiny sections of bare ice. But Balto ran straight and steady, pulling hard against the wind, leading the team across creek after creek and lagoon after lagoon.

Inside Maynard Columbus Hospital in Nome, Dr. Welch moved between the beds. The sound of thick, wet coughing filled the air. The faces on the pillows were red and flushed with fever. Dr. Welch paused and checked a little girl's mouth. A thick, sticky web stretched across the back of her throat. Dr. Welch clenched his jaw. She needed

the antitoxin—all of them did—or she would die. There was nothing he could do except wipe her hot face and lift her head when the terrible cough shook her frame. Dr. Welch could only hope that the serum would arrive soon.

Out on the trail, the sled team was running as fast as they could. The storm was still howling. Surely it can't grow any worse, Gunnar thought. He didn't know just how wrong he was.

CHAPTER 9

No Obstacle Too Great!

As the team plowed its way down the trail, the blizzard winds were blowing almost eighty miles an hour. At the head of the line, Balto struggled to keep pulling. The dogs were jerked around as the wind gusted first one way, then the other. The sled rocked back and forth.

They'd missed the roadhouse at Solomon, Gunnar realized. It was behind them. There wouldn't be any rest. There wouldn't be any hot coffee for him or salmon for the tired team. There was only the darkness and screaming winds and numbing fingers and creeping, punishing cold.

Suddenly, a strong gust lifted the sled and flipped it over, pulling the dogs right off their feet. Gunnar and the team landed in a pile, buried in snow. Balto scrambled to his feet, tangled in his harness. He stood quietly in the raging wind while Gunnar wearily took his gloves off and sorted out the lines.

Again and again, the sled blew off the trail, carrying the dogs with it. The dogs were aching with cold and weariness. Gunnar risked frozen fingers every time he took his gloves off to untangle the harnesses.

Then, a monstrous burst of wind slammed into the dogs. The sled flipped over and over, dragging the dogs with it. Gunnar tumbled into a drift. Panting, he dragged himself out and felt his way through the darkness to the team.

The sled was overturned in a snowbank. The dogs were tangled in their harnesses again, lying in a heap on top of one another. Slowly, Gunnar pulled the sled out and set it upright on its runners. He led the dogs out of the snowbank and untangled their harnesses.

Then he ran his hands over the sled to check that the serum crate was still secured. His hands moved down smooth wood. Then up and down again. Something was wrong.

The crate was gone.

Frantically, Gunnar searched the sled. No crate. No serum. It must have flown off when the sled was upended. Gunnar dropped to his knees, heart pounding, and felt all around the sled in the deep snow. He cursed the dark and the storm that blocked his vision. How could the team have come so far in this blizzard only to lose the serum?

Gunnar's breath was ragged. He crawled back and forth along the trail, hoping his fingers would brush against the cloth that wrapped the wooden crate. Nothing.

The dogs stood patiently, bracing themselves against the wind. Their eyes were almost closed against the ice beating against their faces. Gunnar ripped his gloves off and thrust his hands into the freezing snow. He raked

through the snowbanks.

Finally, his knuckles knocked against something hard. The crate! He threw himself on it. Almost sobbing with relief, Gunnar grabbed the serum and pulled it from the snow. He tied it to the sled with the tightest knots he could manage.

"Hike!" he shouted to Balto. The dog pulled hard into the wind. They were once again on their way to Port Safety.

CHAPTER 10

A Change in the Plan

Around three o'clock in the morning, the dogs could tell that rest was ahead. As soon as the roadhouse at Port Safety appeared on the curve of the trail, Balto picked up his speed. The whole team needed a break. Their feet were aching and crusted with ice and their joints were beginning to stiffen.

But as the team neared the dark bulk of the roadhouse, Gunnar squinted through the snow. Something was wrong. Warm, orange light should have been spilling from the windows and onto the snow. It was always a welcome sight to tired drivers coming down the trail. These windows were dark. There was no sign of Ed Rohn, the final driver, watching from the window or standing in the doorway.

Ed was tucked deep into furs inside, fast asleep. No team was harnessed out front.

Gunnar didn't know that a message had been sent from the town leaders. Through the telephone line that linked Nome to the roadhouses at Port Safety and Solomon, the information was passed: The storm was growing too dangerous. All drivers should shelter in place until it passed. The message had been waiting for Gunnar at the Solomon roadhouse, but he had never arrived.

When Ed got the message, he agreed with the town leaders. No one should be driving in this storm. So, Ed put his dogs to bed and went to sleep.

Gunnar had a decision to make. He could wake up Ed and give him the serum. But Ed would need to hitch up his dogs and prepare his sled. This would all take time. And every minute was a minute that a child might not have the medicine they needed.

Besides, the wind wasn't as bad now. And Balto and the team couldn't just stand in the cold. They had to keep moving to stay warm. Nome was only twenty-five miles away.

Balto looked up at Gunnar. Snow crusted his furry face but his black eyes were bright and steady. He stood quietly, his strong legs braced against the wind. He'd led the team through the blizzard. He'd been blown off his feet and thrown into snowbanks. He'd crossed Topkok Mountain in the dark. He'd found the trail when it was lost. He was a lead dog now and he knew Gunnar needed him.

Gunnar rubbed Balto between his ears. "Can you take us to Nome, buddy?" he asked. Balto pressed his head against Gunnar's hand and wagged his tail. Behind him, the team waited patiently, their eyes half-closed against the wind.

Gunnar straightened and stepped back onto the sled. He grasped the handlebar. "Hike!" he shouted. The team leaned into their harnesses. Gunnar had asked, and his lead dog had answered. The race was back on.

CHAPTER 11

Balto Saves the Day

The streets of Nome were always quiet during the dark, frigid Arctic dawn. Still, on February 2, a few people were out, even at 5:30 in the morning. They were hurrying along the sidewalks, buried deep in their fur parkas. The wind was dying down. The buildings on Front Street were half hidden in snowdrifts from the blizzard.

Suddenly, a small, dark smudge appeared far out on the trail that led into the town. After a few moments, the people on the street could tell it was a sled dog team. The sight of the team grew larger and larger as they neared Front Street, with a big, black dog running at the front.

The serum had arrived. Someone ran for Dr. Welch. Gunnar, covered in snow, pulled up in front of the Miners & Merchants Bank. He stepped off the sled. Legs shaking with exhaustion, he staggered toward Balto. "Fine dog," he mumbled. Then he fainted.

*   *   *

Minutes after the team's arrival, Dr. Welch was unwrapping the serum. Not one bottle was broken. Dr. Welch thawed the serum until it was the correct temperature. Then he got right to work, injecting the sickest children

with the antitoxin that morning.

By late in the evening, Dr. Welch had already used much of the 300,000 units of the serum. People began receiving second doses. The spread of the disease was halted.

The relay had been a wild success, with 150 dogs and twenty drivers covering 674 miles over five and a half days. The journey from Nenana to Nome normally took twenty-five days. Gunnar and his team had run fifty-three miles without a break to reach the finish line.

Later, Gunnar told the story of the

final twenty miles. The trail had taken them along the beach, and although the wind had dropped, the team was stiff with cold. Gunnar's fingers were numb with frostbite. Balto kept running, straight and true, plowing through heavy drifts of snow. When Gunnar saw the cross above St. Joseph's Church, he knew they had made it.

The medicine dosing went ahead. Anyone showing symptoms was given the serum.

On February 15, a second crate of serum arrived by dogsled, in another blizzard. It, too, had been delivered by train to Nenana and relayed over the trail. This time, the final driver was Ed Rohn. Finally, on February 21, the quarantine was lifted. The crisis was over.

CHAPTER 12

The Rest Is History

Balto became an instant celebrity. President Calvin Coolidge sent a message praising the dogs and the drivers. The United States Senate put out a note of thanks. Newspaper and radio reporters had breathlessly followed the progress of the serum run. Now they wanted to write about the famous dog who had saved Nome. Though 150 dogs had been a part of the relay and twenty drivers had risked their lives, the press needed one person and one dog to focus on. That made the story they were telling easier for people to understand. So Gunnar and Balto were made into the stars of the relay.

Gunnar took Balto on a tour of the United States. The dog was celebrated everywhere he went. He even appeared in a Hollywood movie called *Balto's*

Race to Nome. Movie stars wanted to have their picture taken with him. Wreaths of flowers were placed around his neck.

For nine months, Gunnar and Balto traveled across the country so that people could meet the hero dog who saved Nome. Balto was friendly and patient at each stop. He loved people.

Leonhard Seppala was not happy with Balto's fame. He felt like his lead dog, Togo, was not receiving the attention he deserved for his part in the relay. His team had run the longest distance, after all. At events, Leonhard loudly declared that Togo was the real hero of the Nome relay.

On December 16, eleven months after the serum run, Gunnar and Balto stood before a crowd in New York

City's Central Park. Gunnar wore his fur parka and fur pants. Balto panted patiently. To cheers and applause, a cloth was whisked off the top of a bronze statue of Balto himself, his ears perked, eyes looking ahead. Balto paid little attention to the sculpture. He was more interested in trying to fight two other sled dogs who were in the crowd.

After the tour, Gunnar returned to his old life in Nome. Balto and the team stayed behind. For a time, they were kept in a room in a sideshow in Los Angeles. The dogs weren't happy there, and a businessman named George Kimble noticed. He raised two thousand dollars to bring the dogs to the Brookside Zoo in Cleveland, Ohio.

In March of 1927, two years after the relay, Balto and six of his fellow sled dogs paraded through the streets of Cleveland while thousands of people cheered. They spent the rest of their

days living in comfort at the zoo. Balto died peacefully on March 14, 1933. He was fourteen years old.

Balto's heroism and the bravery of all the drivers and dogs on the serum run were never forgotten. Every year, the Iditarod Trail Sled Dog Race is run from Anchorage to Nome over much of the same route that Balto, Blackie, Togo, Wild Bill, Leonhard, Charlie, Gunnar, and the other drivers and dogs ran. The race was created in 1973 in their memory.

On the first Saturday in March, drivers and sled dog teams begin their run of just under a thousand miles. Their modern sleds and harnesses still look very much like those Leonhard, Gunnar, and their teams used. And their dogs still love to run. They sleep curled on beds of straw in the snow, just as Togo and Balto did.

The finish line, strung with lights and banners, stretches across Front Street, on the same ground that Balto and Gunnar crossed.

Many of the dogs who run across that finish line are the descendants of the serum run dogs. In their blood, they carry the spirit of the huskies who saved Nome. In their bones, they carry that same love of the trail.

Note to Readers

Some scenes in this book have been fictionalized. While the facts and details of the story are true, the emotions and inner thoughts of the historical figures in this book have been imagined by the author.

Acknowledgments

I would like to thank the authors Gay and Laney Salisbury for their book *The Cruelest Miles* (W. W. Norton & Company, 2003), which was an invaluable resource during the writing of this book.

I'd also like to express my appreciation to sled dog breeder and trainer Howard M. Thompson of Sno-Trek Sled Dog Adventures in Mondovi, Wisconsin, for answering many questions about the raising and training of today's sled dogs.

Timeline

1919
Balto is born.

January 27, 1925
The serum relay begins with Wild Bill Shannon and Blackie as the first driver and lead dog.

January 20, 1925
In Nome, Dr. Curtis Welch diagnoses the outbreak's first case of diphtheria.

March 19, 1927
Balto and six of his fellow sled dogs parade through the streets of Cleveland, Ohio, on their way to their new home at the Brookside Zoo.

March 14, 1933
Balto dies peacefully in Cleveland at the age of fourteen.

January 31, 1925
Leonhard Seppala and lead dog Togo receive the serum and begin their 91-mile run.

February 2, 1925
The serum relay ends with Gunnar Kaasen and Balto as the last driver and lead dog.

March 21, 1925
Gunnar and Balto arrive in Seattle, Washington, to begin their mainland tour.

December 16, 1925
The statue of Balto is unveiled in New York's Central Park.

March 3, 1973
The first modern Iditarod Trail Sled Dog Race is run.

Biographies

Gunnar Kaasen

Gunnar Kaasen was born in Norway in 1882 and came to Nome in search of gold in 1904. He worked as a sled dog driver hauling freight. After the 1925 serum run, Gunnar returned to Nome and went back to his old job and life. Gunnar retired in 1950. He moved to Everett, Washington, in 1952 with his wife, Anna. Gunnar lived there until his death on November 27, 1960.

Leonhard Seppala

Born in Norway in 1877, Leonhard found his way to Nome in 1900, looking for gold. He began raising and training sled dogs. In 1915, he won the All-Alaska Sweepstakes, Alaska's biggest sled dog race. One of Alaska's best-known drivers, Leonhard was a key figure in the 1925 serum run. He continued racing and working in Alaska for many more years. In 1947, Leonhard moved to Seattle, where he died on January 28, 1967. His ashes were scattered along the Iditarod Trail that he had run so many times.

About the Author and Illustrator

 Emma Carlson Berne is the author of many books of history and historical fiction for young readers. She lives in Cincinnati, Ohio, with her husband and three little boys. Emma likes to horseback ride, hike, camp, and read to her sons.

 Francesca Rosa is an Italian illustrator based in Milan with her husband Lorenzo and two little bunnies, Moka and Cookie. Her love for animals brought her to draw them alongside children as the main characters of her stories. She specializes in children's books and she has collaborated with many famous publishers around the world. In her spare time, Francesca loves to create pottery and watch TV.

Recommended Reading

Blake, Robert J. *Togo.* New York: Philomel Books, 2002.

Cary, Bob. *Born to Pull: The Glory of Sled Dogs.* Minneapolis, MN: University of Minnesota Press, 2009.

Miller, Debbie S. *The Great Serum Race: Blazing the Iditarod Trail.* New York: Walker & Co, 2002.